Contents

Getting ready

Christmas is coming!

How do you

get ready?

Sam and Mia decorate.

They hang lights on a tree.

6

Joe and Ana bake.
They help Dad
make biscuits.

8

Liam helps others.

He serves food at a shelter.

La! Gabby sings.
She knows the words
to lots of carols.

Time with family

Maria goes to church.

She sits with her family.

Katie visits
her family.
She goes to
Grandma's house.

Georgia gives presents.

She wraps a toy for her sister.

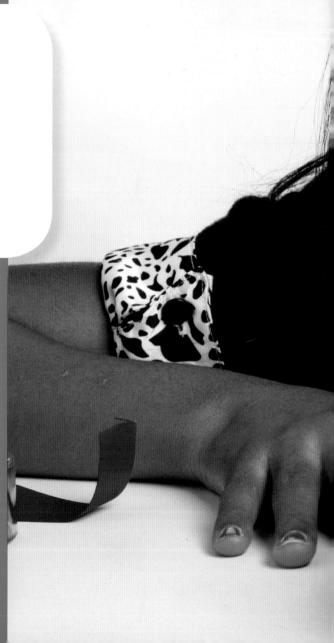

Counting the days

Three, two, one!

James counts down the days.

How do you celebrate Christmas?

Glossary

carol song people sing at Christmas

celebrate honour a special event

Christmas event Christians celebrate to honour the birth of Jesus

church place people go to pray, sing and worship

shelter place that helps people by giving them food and somewhere to sleep if they have nowhere else that is safe to go to

wrap put paper or cloth around a present

Read more

Festivals (Picture This!), Rebecca Rissman
(Raintree, 2013)

Grandparents (Families), Rebecca Rissman
(Raintree, 2012)

Websites

www.naturedetectives.org.uk/winter/
Download winter wildlife ID sheets, pick up some
great snowy-weather-game ideas and discover all the
fun you can have with winter sticks!

www.wildlifewatch.org.uk/
Explore the Wildlife Trust's wildlife watch website and
get busy this winter spotting interesting winter plants
and animals living near by! Follow badger's blog
for great wildlife spotting tips and some fascinating
photographs.

Index